Milkshakes and Lassi

ROMAIN PAGES PUBLISHING

Contents

Milkshakes and Lassi

by **Cécile LE HINGRAT**

Photographs: Jean-Pierre DUVAL

ROMAIN PAGES PUBLISHING

Introduction

Milkshake, shaken, not stirred… what a programme! These are dairy-based beverages, blends of fresh fruit, ice cubes, ice cream or sherbet, syrup, and other ingredients. The blending makes for a light, creamy consistency, which accounts for their popularity in recent decades.

Lassi comes directly from India and is made from blended or fermented yogurt. Lassi is a little thicker than a milkshake, and works well with exotic and refined flavours. Nutritionally speaking, both milkshakes and lassi are known for being very nourishing and sweet. They seduce the most extreme food lovers with whipped cream, melted chocolate and ice cream. But they can also be very low fat, with few calories, if you make them with fresh fruit, milk, low-fat yogurt and crushed ice… and you do not add too much sugar!

The forty-four recipes in this book are sorted into five categories, from the most classic milkshakes and lassi (vanilla, chocolate, strawberry, coffee, etc.) to the most surprising (rum-based, carrot/ginger/cumin, chervil and broad bean, and more). The first four chapters (classic, fruit-based, original and with spirits) cover sweet milkshakes and lassi. The last, however, covers savoury milkshakes and lassi, which are perfect to serve as an appetizer. The milkshakes and lassi made with spirits are for adults, only, but children will love others that marry fruit and spices, which are ideal for snack!

In these pages, the "Did you know?" and "Tips and Tricks" sidebars teach you how to choose fruits and vegetables, what eating them contributes to your diet, and how to store them. The section called "Twists" gives recipe variations (fewer calories, more or less elaborate, etc.).

Finally, milkshakes and lassi are also good because they look good! Serve them in pretty glasses, with straws; have fun mixing colours; sprinkle with powdered chocolate or icing sugar; and serve with finger food… you will find the recipes in this book as well (try the parmesan lolly, rolled biscuits, almond tuiles, and more). Here are a few recommendations before you begin blending.

Some advice
before getting started…

Equipment
Use a blender with a large glass bowl and several blending speeds. Be careful, the blade has to be resistant enough to blend frozen ingredients, ice cream and ice cubes. If you do not have a blender, you can use a handheld blender to make the milkshakes and lassi whose ingredients are soft enough (in this case, never use frozen ingredients). Only add the ice cubes or crushed ice after blending, to cool down the mixture. The result is not quite the same, but when you really, really want a milkshake or a lassi, it will do.

In the recipes, we suggest blending for about 30 seconds. This duration can vary a little depending on the brand of blender you are using; read the manufacturer's instructions for more details. The trick to knowing when to stop the blending is that you no longer hear the noise of ice cubes in the blender and the preparation appears smooth and frothy. This means your milkshake or lassi is ready for serving.

Start mixing at a slow speed, and increase the speed little by little, ending at the maximum speed for a few seconds.

Ingredients
There is no secret to a good milkshake or lassi: you need quality ingredients! The fruit and vegetables have to be ripe. Choose seasonal ingredients: this is important because they are flavourful and juicy. If you want to eat summer fruit all year long, you can freeze it in pieces and use them as is in your blender. Prefer organically grown fruit and vegetables, particularly if you are using the zest or the skin. If you prepare the ingredients ahead of time, beware of fruit and vegetables that turn brown when exposed to the air: apples, pears, bananas, avocados, and the like. Sprinkle them with some lemon juice and keep them in a cool, dark place. Finally, if you have time, make the ice cream, sherbet and yogurts yourself (you will find recipes in our books Homemade Ice Creams and Sherbets and Homemade Yogurt). This can only make your milkshake or lassi all that much better.

Textures
The final consistency you get depends a lot on the recipe:
- Ice cream, which contains milk, will make the milkshake or lassi creamy.
- Banana and avocado will give it a creamy, smooth consistency.

- The quality of the juice found in the fruit and vegetables you use will make the milkshake or lassi more or less liquid.

Adjust the recipes to your taste:
- Thicken the preparation by adding a half yogurt, some fresh cheese, banana (only in sweet milkshakes and lassi) or avocado. If you use these ingredients in small quantities, they will not mask the main flavours. Add them progressively, a little bit at a time, until you get the thickness you want.
- If, on the contrary, you want to make your milkshake or lassi thinner, add milk.

If you like very cold milkshakes and lassi, freeze the ingredients that can be frozen (certain fruits and vegetables, fresh cheese, yogurt, cream, etc.). Once frozen, put them directly in the blender and they will cool your preparation without ice cubes; the latter tend to dilute the mixture.

Service
There are many good reasons, other than just plain fondness of food, to consume your milkshake or lassi immediately, right after it has been blended:
- Once processed, fruits and vegetables quickly lose their vitamins.
- Milkshakes and lassi tend to loose their smoothness with time: the ingredients separate and form layers in the glasses, which is not very appetizing.
- The colour of the final product could change in contact with air and light due to oxidation.

In a word, listen only to your desire and to your children… do not wait a minute longer to taste these delicious milkshakes and lassi!

Ingredients

- 4 scoops vanilla ice cream
- 1 Bourbon vanilla pod
- 20 cl / 6 ¾ fl oz / ⅘ cup milk
- 6 ice cubes

SERVES: 2
PREPARATION TIME: 10 MIN

Little raisin cakes:

- 250 g / 9 oz / 2 cups flour
- 175 g / 6 ¼ oz / ¾ cup butter
- 125 g / 4 ⅓ oz / ⅝ cup sugar
- 3 eggs
- 150 g / 5 ¼ oz / ⅔ cup raisins
- ½ packet baking powder
- 1 pinch salt

MAKES 16 CAKES
PREPARATION TIME: 10 MIN
COOKING TIME: 15 MIN

Bourbon Vanilla

1 . Split the vanilla pod in half lengthwise, scrape out the seeds with the tip of a knife.

2 . Heat the milk in a saucepan with the vanilla pod and its seeds. Bring to a boil. Remove from heat and cool to room temperature.

3 . Remove the vanilla pod from the milk. Put the vanilla-flavoured milk, the vanilla ice cream and the ice cubes in the blender.

4 . Process for about 30 seconds, until you get a creamy mixture.

5 . Serve immediately.

Little Raisin Cakes

1 . Soak the raisins in hot water for 30 minutes until they are plump.

2 . Mix the softened butter with the sugar, using a wooden spoon.

3 . Mix together the flour, a pinch of salt and the baking powder, and then add this mixture to the butter and sugar.

4 . Add the eggs one by one, mixing constantly.

5 . Preheat the oven to 180°C/350°F/gas mark 4.

6 . Drain the raisins, pat dry and flour. Mix them into the batter.

7 . Fill small silicon moulds with batter.

8 . Cook for 10 minutes, then lower the temperature to 150°C/300°F/gas mark 2 and cook for another 5 minutes.

Ingredients

- 4 scoops chocolate ice cream
- 2 tablespoons dark cacao
- 2 tablespoons sugar
- 2 tablespoons white chocolate shavings (optional)
- 20 cl / 6 ¾ fl oz / ⅘ cup milk
- 6 ice cubes

SERVES: 2
PREPARATION TIME: 5 MIN

Rolled "cigarette" biscuits:

- 90 g / 3 ⅛ oz / ¾ cup sifted flour
- 80 g / 2 ¾ oz / generous ¼ cup butter
- 1 teaspoon crème fraîche or double cream
- 150 g / 5 ¼ oz / 1 ⅕ cup powdered milk
- 1 packet vanilla sugar
- 3 egg whites

SERVES: 4
PREPARATION TIME: 10 MIN
COOKING TIME: 15 MIN

Chocolate

1 . Put all the ingredients except the white chocolate in the blender.

2 . Process for about 30 seconds, until you get a thick, creamy mixture.

3 . You can decorate the milkshake with white chocolate slivers.

4 . Serve immediately with rolled biscuits (see below recipe).

Rolled "Cigarette" Biscuits

1 . Mix with a wooden spoon the butter, the sugar and the vanilla sugar.

2 . Add the 3 egg whites little by little, and then the crème fraîche, followed by the flour. Whisk energetically.

3 . Preheat the oven to 240°C/475°F/gas mark 9.

4 . Line a baking dish with greaseproof paper and make about 16 small piles of batter, about 2 cm/¾ inch in diameter.

5 . Bake for 5 minutes.

6 . Remove from the oven and while still warm roll the biscuits around the handle of a wooden spoon.

7 . Allow to cool. Store the biscuits in a metal box.

Twists

You can feel less guilty by making a light version of this milkshake. Just replace two of the four scoops of ice cream with two vanilla yogurts.

Ingredients

- 2 scoops vanilla ice cream
- 2 scoops strawberry sherbet
- 10 strawberries
- 2 tablespoons sugar (or strawberry syrup)
- 20 cl / 6 ¾ fl oz / ⅘ cup milk
- 6 ice cubes

SERVES: 2
PREPARATION TIME: 5 MIN

Strawberry

1 . Wash the strawberries and then remove the stems. Drain a few minutes on paper towels.

2 . Place the strawberries and all the other ingredients in the blender.

3 . Process for about 30 seconds, until you get a frothy mixture.

4 . Serve immediately.

Did you know?

Choose locally grown strawberry varieties over large, less flavourful imported varieties from the Mediterranean or South America. There are as many as 600 strawberry varieties, some of which are produced by local farmers. Typically, the larger the strawberry, the more water it contains. Smaller varieties generally have a more intense flavour.

As Lassi

Replace the 4 scoops of ice cream with 2 yogurts or 20 cl / 6 ¾ fl oz / ⅘ cup churned buttermilk. Add an additional 10 strawberries and 2 tablespoons sugar or strawberry syrup.

Ingredients

- 4 scoops coffee ice cream
- 2 tablespoons sugar
- 30 g / 1 oz meringue, broken into pieces
- 2 tablespoons
- chocolate shavings
- 15 cl / 5 fl oz / ⅔ cup milk
- 5 cl / 1 pint / 2 cups cold espresso
- 6 ice cubes

SERVES: 2
PREPARATION TIME: 5 MIN

Coffee

1 . Place all the ingredients, except the meringue and the chocolate shavings, into the blender.

2 . Process for about 30 seconds, until you get a thick, creamy mixture.

3 . Sprinkle the meringue pieces and the chocolate shavings on top of the milkshake.

4 . Serve immediately.

Did you know?

Coffee is said to have originated in Ethiopia, where there is a fine legend about its discovery. Once there was a forest fire that consumed a coffee tree grove, giving off a delicious aroma, leading those who saw the fire to recuperate the roasted beans, crush them and make them into a drink. And thus coffee was born.

Ingredients

Dark chocolate:

- 2 scoops dark chocolate
  ice cream
- 1 tablespoon sugar
- 5 cl / 1 ⅔ fl oz /
  3 ⅓ tablespoons milk
- 3 ice cubes

White chocolate:

- 2 scoops white chocolate
  ice cream
- 5 cl / 1 ⅔ fl oz /
  3 ⅓ tablespoons milk
- 6 ice cubes

SERVES: 2 TO 3
PREPARATION TIME: 10 MIN

Dark chocolate discs:

- 100 g / 3 ½ oz
  dark chocolate

SERVES: 2 TO 3
PREPARATION TIME: 10 MIN
SET ASIDE: 1 HR

Double chocolate

1 . Make the two milkshakes separately.

2 . Place all the dark chocolate milkshake ingredients in the blender.

3 . Process for about 30 seconds, until you get a frothy mixture.

4 . Do the same for the white chocolate mixture.

5 . Pour one of them in the serving glass, gently top with a dark chocolate disc (see the below recipe) and pour in the other milkshake.

6 . Serve immediately.

Dark Chocolate Discs

1 . Melt the dark chocolate over a water bath.

2 . On a piece of parchment paper, shape discs the diameter of your glass.

3 . Smooth the surface and allow to dry for an hour at room temperature.

Twists

Another, simpler option, consists of serving the two milkshakes separately in two small glasses. Food lovers can add orange marmalade and/or melted chocolate at the bottom of the glass, and then top with whipped cream and sprinkle with bitter cacao powder.

Ingredients

- 4 scoops fior di latte ice cream (see Tips and Tricks, below)
- 2 ripe bananas
- 2 tablespoons sugar
- 1 pinch four-spice powder (cloves, pepper, cinnamon, nutmeg)
- 1 scant teaspoon curcuma
- 20 cl / 6 ¾ fl oz / ⅘ cup milk
- 1 teaspoon lemon juice
- 6 ice cubes

SERVES: 2
PREPARATION TIME: 5 MIN

Spicy Curcuma Banana

1 . Peel the bananas and slice. Brush them with lemon juice so they do not turn brown.

2 . Place the bananas and all the other ingredients in the blender.

3 . Process for about 30 seconds, until you get a thick, creamy mixture.

4 . Serve immediately.

Did you know?

Curcuma comes from Southern Asia. It is used a lot in India, where it is used in curries. It has a number of uses and virtues, and traditional medicine recommends it to treat digestive problems, gastric ulcers, and skin ailments. It is also used as an orange-yellow dye, to colour monks' robes, for example.

Tips and Tricks

Fior di latte ice cream comes from Italy. You can make it yourself in an ice cream machine, using the following ingredients: 50 cl / 1 pint / 2 cups milk, 50 cl / 1 pint / 2 cups whole crème fraîche, 100 g / 3 ½ oz / ½ cup icing sugar, a packet of vanilla sugar, 1 egg white beaten until stiff, 1 pinch salt.

Ingredients

- 2 scoops vanilla ice cream
- 2 scoops pear sherbet
- 2 pears
- 1 pinch Sichuan pepper
- 20 cl / 6 ¾ fl oz / ⅘ cup milk
- juice of ½ lemon
- 6 ice cubes

SERVES: 2
PREPARATION TIME: 5 MIN

Almond tuiles:

- 50 g / 1 ¾ oz / 1/4 cup sugar
- 30 g / 1 oz / ⅛ cup butter
- 20 g / ⅔ oz / 2 tablespoons flour
- 20 g / ⅔ oz / ¼ cup almond slivers
- 1 egg white

MAKES 4 LARGE TUILES
PREPARATION TIME: 10 MIN
COOKING TIME: 10 MIN

Sichuan Pear

1 . Peel the pears, cut into quarters and remove the seeds and the core. Cut the pears into pieces. Brush with lemon juice so they do not turn brown.

2 . Place the pear pieces and all the other ingredients in the blender.

3 . Process for about 30 seconds, until you get a frothy mixture.

4 . Serve immediately with almond tuiles (see below recipe).

Almond Tuiles

1 . Preheat the oven to 180°C/350°F/gas mark 4.

2 . Beat the egg white slightly, until it is frothy.

3 . Add the softened butter, the sugar, the almonds and the flour.

4 . Line a baking sheet with greaseproof paper and top with small piles of the batter. Space them far enough apart so they do not run together when they cook.

5 . Bake for about 10 minutes.

6 . Remove from the oven and while they are still warm, drape them over a rolling pin or a glass bottle, so they look like roof tiles (*tuiles*). Cool. Store the tuiles in a metal box.

Ingredients

- 2 scoops peach sherbet
- 1 scoop apricot sherbet
- 1 scoop vanilla ice cream
- 2 peaches
- 2 apricots
- 2 star anise
- 20 cl / 6 ¾ fl oz / ⅘ cup milk
- 6 ice cubes

SERVES: **2**
PREPARATION TIME: **5** MIN
COOKING TIME: **10** MIN

Peach-Apricot with Star Anise

1 . Heat the milk in a saucepan with the star anise. Bring to a boil.

2 . Remove from heat and cool to room temperature. Remove the star anise from the milk (you can throw them away or compost them).

4 . Peel and pit the peaches and the apricots.

5 . Place the flavoured milk, the fruit and all the other ingredients in the blender.

6 . Process for about 30 seconds, until you get a thick, creamy mixture.

7 . Serve immediately.

Did you know?

Star anise is a medicinal plant used to fight gastrointestinal ailments (boating, wind, flatulence), and also against coughs, colds and bad breath!

As Lassi

Replace the 4 scoops of ice cream with 2 yogurts or 20 cl / 6 ¾ fl oz / ⅘ cup churned buttermilk. Add 1 peach and 4 tablespoons sugar (or peach or apricot syrup).

20

Ingredients

- 4 scoops coconut ice cream
- 4 tablespoons grated coconut
- 50 g / 1 3/4 oz dark chocolate
- 2 tablespoons sugar
- 10 cl / 3 1/3 fl oz / 2/5 cup coconut milk
- 10 cl / 3 1/3 fl oz / 2/5 cup milk
- 6 ice cubes

SERVES: **2**
PREPARATION TIME: **10** MIN
SET ASIDE: **15** MIN

1 . Melt the dark chocolate in a water bath and pour into the bottom of serving glasses. Set aside at room temperature for 15 minutes to harden.

2 . Place all the other ingredients in the blender.

3 . Process for about 30 seconds, until you get a creamy mixture.

4 . Pour delicately onto the chocolate preparation.

5 . Serve immediately.

Did you know?

Choosing a coconut should not be taken lightly: the fruit should be heavy, full, and have no cracks. Its eyes (the three cavities found on the shell) should be intact and not be mouldy. Once open, coconuts oxidise quickly and should be stored in cold water to avoid contact with the air. A suggestion: grate it and store it in a hermetically sealed recipient so that you can use it for several months.

As Lassi

Replace the 4 scoops of ice cream with 2 yogurts or 20 cl / 6 3/4 fl oz / 4/5 cup churned buttermilk. Replace the milk with 10 cl / 3 1/3 fl oz / 2/5 cup coconut milk (making 20 cl / 6 3/4 fl oz / 4/5 cup in total). Add 2 tablespoons castor sugar.

- 3 scoops pineapple sherbet
- 1 scoop vanilla ice cream
- 1 mango
- 1/2 pineapple
- 1 tablespoon brown sugar
- 20 cl / 6 3/4 fl oz / 4/5 cup milk
- 6 ice cubes

SERVES: 2
PREPARATION TIME: 10 MIN

Pineapple Mango

1 . Peel the mango and cut in two lengthwise to remove the pit. Then cut it into medium-sized pieces.

2 . Remove the skin, the eyes and the hard core from the half pineapple. Then cut it into medium-sized pieces.

3 . Place the mango and pineapple pieces and all the other ingredients in the blender.

4 . Process for about 30 seconds, until you get a frothy mixture.

5 . Serve immediately.

Did you know?

True or false? Pineapple burns fat. Unfortunately, this is false. Eating pineapples does not influence you body fat. They are, however, excellent for the digestion, make your skin shine, and provide a multitude of vitamins!

As Lassi

Remplacez les 4 boules de glace par 2 yaourts ou 20 cl de lait ribot. Remplacez le 1/2 ananas par 1 petit ananas entier. Ajoutez 2 cuillères à soupe de sucre.

Ingredients

- 2 scoops vanilla ice cream
- 4 tablespoons sweetened chestnut purée (around 200 g / 7oz)
- 6 chestnuts (large, weighing about 60 g / 2 oz)
- 2 tablespoons
- candied chestnut pieces
- 30 cl / 10 fl oz / 1 ¼ cup milk
- 6 ice cubes

SERVES: 2
PREPARATION TIME: 5 MIN

Vanilla Chestnut

1 . Put all the ingredients except the candied chestnut pieces into the blender.

2 . Process for about 30 seconds, until you get a creamy mixture.

3 . Sprinkle the milkshake with candied chestnut pieces and serve immediately.

Did you know?

Did you know that chestnuts were, for a long time, a staple food in regions like north-western France, the Massif Central, Corsica, Portugal and northern Italy? In the countryside, chestnuts often replaced wheat and other grains, and the chestnut tree was called a "bread tree".

Twists

If you really love chestnuts, use chestnut ice cream instead of vanilla ice cream.

Pistachio Raspberry

1 . Wash and pat dry the raspberries.

2 . Place the raspberries, the pistachio ice cream, the raspberry syrup, the milk and the ice cubes in the blender.

3 . Process for about 30 seconds, until you get a thick, creamy mixture.

4 . Chop the pistachios and sprinkle onto each milkshake.

5 . Serve immediately.

- 4 scoops pistachio ice cream
- 200 g / 7 oz raspberries (fresh or frozen)
- 50 g / 1 ¾ oz / ½ cup unsalted pistachios
- 2 tablespoons raspberry syrup
- 20 cl / 6 ¾ fl oz / ⅘ cup milk
- 6 ice cubes

SERVES: 2
PREPARATION TIME: 5 MIN

Tips and Tricks

If you can only find salted pistachios, shell them and boil them for 1 minute. Drain and leave them to dry a few hours in the sun. This gets rid of the salt, and you can use them for your desserts.

Ingredients

- 2 scoops vanilla ice cream
- 2 scoops cantaloupe sherbet
- 1 small cantaloupe (about 250 g / 9 oz)
- 1 small piece fresh ginger
- 1/2 teaspoon ground ginger
- 20 cl / 6 3/4 fl oz / 4/5 cup milk
- 6 ice cubes

SERVES: 2
PREPARATION TIME: 5 MIN

Candied ginger:

- 250 g / 9 oz fresh ginger
- 400 g / 14 oz / 2 cups sugar
- sugar for coating

SERVES: 10
PREPARATION TIME: 15 MIN
AHEAD OF TIME: 6 DAYS
COOKING TIME: 35 MIN

Ginger Cantaloupe

1 . Peel and seed the cantaloupe. Peel the fresh ginger. Cut them both into small pieces.

2 . Place the cantaloupe and ginger pieces with all the other ingredients in the blender.

3 . Process for about 30 seconds, until you get a thick, creamy mixture.

4 . Serve immediately with a skewer of candied ginger (see below recipe) and fresh cantaloupe.

Candied ginger

1 . Peel the fresh ginger. Cut it into very thin slices using a mandoline or a very sharp knife.

2 . Soak in cold water for one hour.

3 . Wash the ginger, place in a saucepan and cover with fresh cold water. Boil for 5 minutes. Drain and repeat the operation three times.

4 . Mix the sugar with 250 cl/8 1/2 fl oz/1 cup water and bring to a boil. Pour this syrup onto the ginger. Remove from heat, cover and set aside for 12 hours.

5 . Drain the ginger. Recuperate the syrup and bring to a boil for 10 minutes. Pour the boiling syrup onto the ginger, cover and set aside for another two days.

6 . Boil the mixture for 5 minutes and set aside for another three days.

7 . Drain the ginger and spread it out on greaseproof paper. Sprinkle with sugar.

8 . Store in a dry place.

Ingredients

- 4 scoops apple sherbet
- 1 apple
- 1 quince
- 1 tablespoon
- dulce de leche (see below recipe)
- $1/4$ teaspoon ground cinnamon
- 20 cl / 6 $3/4$ fl oz / $4/5$ cup custard sauce
- 6 ice cubes

SERVES: 2
PREPARATION TIME: 10 MIN
COOKING TIME: 15 MIN

Dulce de leche:

- 1 can unsweetened condensed milk

MAKES 1 CAN
PREPARATION TIME: 1 MIN
COOKING TIME: 2 HRS

Apple and quince with dulce de leche

1 . Peel the quince and the apple, cut into quarters, remove the cores and cut into large cubes.

2 . Cook in boiling water for 15 minutes. Drain the fruit and cool to room temperature.

3 . Place the fruit with all the other ingredients in the blen der.

4 . Process for about 30 seconds, until you get a thick, creamy mixture.

5 . Serve immediately.

Dulce de leche

1 . Bring some water to boil in a large pot. Put the can of concentrated milk, whole, still closed, directly in the boiling water and simmer for 2 hours. The can must stay covered with water.

2 . Remove the can from the water and cook to room temperature and then refrigerate.

3 . Open and enjoy!

- 4 scoops nougat ice cream
- 2 bananas
- 4 dates
- 2 tablespoons raisins
- 1 tablespoon ground almonds
- 20 cl / 6 ¾ fl oz / ⅘ cup churned buttermilk
- 6 ice cubes

SERVES: **2**
PREPARATION TIME: **10 MIN**

Banana and Dried Fruit Lassi

1 . Peel the bananas. Pit the dates. Cut the fruit into pieces.

2 . Place the fruit with all the other ingredients in the blender.

3 . Process for about 30 seconds, until you get a thick, creamy mixture.

4 . Serve immediately.

Did you know?

Buttermilk is the liquid you get when cream is churned into butter. It is called babeurre in Brittany, guinse in northern France, laban in Arabic countries, and lassi in India.

Twists

You can replace the raisins and powdered almonds with your choice of dried fruit: apricots, pears, prunes, ground hazelnuts, etc. You can also replace the nougat ice cream with pistachio ice cream.

Honey Apple and Speculaas

- 2 scoops nougat ice cream
- 2 scoops apple sherbet
- 1 Granny Smith apple
- 1 Golden apple
- 4 speculaas shortcrust biscuits
- 2 tablespoons acacia honey
- 20 cl / 6 ¾ fl oz / ⅘ cup milk
- 6 ice cubes

SERVES: 2
PREPARATION TIME: 10 MIN

1 . Peel and core the apples. Then cut it into medium-sized pieces.

2 . Put the fruit with all the other ingredients, except the biscuits, in the blender.

3 . Process for about 30 seconds, until you get a thick, creamy mixture.

4 . Crush the biscuits in a mortar. Sprinkle the milkshake with crushed speculaas.

5 . Serve immediately.

Did you know?

Speculaas or speculoos in France are small shortcrust spice biscuits that are very crunchy, and traditionally made in northern France, Belgium and the Netherlands for St. Nicholas' Eve. Their distinctive flavour comes from the brown sugar and the spices they contain: cinnamon, nutmeg, cloves and sometimes ginger. The name speculaas comes from the latin speculum, which means mirror and refers to the earlier tradition of using a wooden stamp to imprint images in the biscuits.

As Lassi

Replace the 4 scoops of ice cream with 2 yogurts or 20 cl / 6 ¾ fl oz / ⅘ cup churned buttermilk. Add 2 tablespoons of apple syrup.

- 4 scoops vanilla ice cream
- 4 carrots
- 1/2 avocado
- 3 tablespoons maple syrup
- 1 pinch nutmeg
- 20 cl / 6 3/4 fl oz / 4/5 cup milk
- 6 ice cubes

SERVES: 2
PREPARATION TIME: 10 MIN

Carrot and Maple Syrup with Nutmeg

1 . Peel the half avocado and remove the pit. Cut into medium-sized pieces.

2 . Wash and peel the carrots. Juice them in a centrifuge juicer.

3 . Put the avocado, 20 cl / 6 3/4 fl oz / 4/5 cup carrot juice and other ingredients in the blender.

4 . Process for about 30 seconds, until you get a frothy mixture.

5 . Serve immediately.

Did you know?

Maple syrup is made from maple sap, collected in spring by tapping through the tree's bark to extract the sap, which is then concentrated by boiling it down. The sap contains about 2% to 3% sugar. In spring, this sugar rises from the roots, just under the tree's bark, giving the tree energy. The tree sap changes further into the sugar season. This change gives the syrup a bitter taste, marking the end of the season. Maple syrup primarily comes from Canada, particularly in Québec, with some production in the north-eastern United States.

Ingredients

- 10 whole almonds
- 2 tablespoons ground almonds
- 2 teaspoons crème fraîche or double cream
- 5 cl / 1 ⅔ fl oz / 3 generous tablespoons orgeat syrup
- 20 cl / 6 ¾ fl oz / ⅘ cup milk
- 6 ice cubes

SERVES: 2
PREPARATION TIME: 10 MIN

Almond

1 . Shell the whole almonds and crush them with a mortar and pestle. Set aside for decorating the milkshakes.

2 . Put all the ingredients, except the crushed almonds, into the blender and process for about 30 seconds, until you get a frothy mixture.

3 . Sprinkle the crushed almonds onto the milkshakes.

4 . Serve immediately.

Tips and Tricks

Put a few almonds into your children's pockets before they go to school. These nuts are an invigorating snack and their high mineral content makes them excellent for healthy bones.

As Lassi

Replace the cream and half the milk with 2 yogurts or 20 cl / 6 ¾ fl oz / ⅘ cup churned buttermilk.

Mint Chocolate

Ingredients

- 2 scoops of mint chocolate chip ice cream
- 2 scoops chocolate ice cream
- 2 tablespoons mint syrup
- 1 sprig fresh mint (optional)
- 20 cl / 6 ¾ fl oz / ⁴⁄₅ cup milk
- 6 ice cubes

SERVES: 2
PREPARATION TIME: 5 MIN

1 . Put all the ingredients in the blender.

2 . Process for about 30 seconds, until you get a frothy mixture.

3 . Decorate with a sprig of mint.

4 . Serve immediately.

Did you know?

The chocolate we eat comes from West Africa (Ivory Coast), Southeast Asia (Indonesia) or South America (Brazil). No matter what people say, eating it is good for you! It contains several substances that can affect your mood, and even be antidepressant and relaxing. It is also very rich in minerals: magnesium, calcium, iron, phosphorus… and it contains antioxidants (vitamin E), which slow down the ageing process.

Twists

If you want a less sweet milkshake, use two tablespoons of fresh mint leaves instead of the mint syrup.

Ingredients

- 2 scoops coffee ice cream
- 2 scoops chocolate ice cream
- 5 cl / 1 ²/₃ fl oz / 3 generous tablespoons cold espresso
- 2 tablespoons bitter cacao powder
- 2 tablespoons sugar
- 3 tablespoons
- mascarpone
- 20 cl / 6 ³/₄ fl oz / ⁴/₅ cup milk
- 6 ice cubes

SERVES: 2
PREPARATION TIME: 10 MIN

Tiramisu

1 . Put all the ingredients, except the cacao, in the blender.

2 . Process for about 30 seconds, until you get a creamy mixture.

3 . Sprinkle the milkshakes with cacao.

4 . Serve immediately.

Did you know?

There are over sixty varieties of coffee. These can be divided into three main categories: arabica, robusta and liberica. Arabica is cultivated in South America (Brazil and Colombia), and is considered to be the best quality. Robusta is imported from Africa. It is average in quality, and has a slightly bitter, strong, tonic taste. Liberica is mediocre and is mainly consumed where it is produced.

Chocolate and Hazelnut

- 4 scoops hazelnut (or praline) ice cream
- 2 tablespoons chocolate and hazelnut spread
- 2 teaspoons shelled hazelnuts
- 20 cl / 6 ¾ fl oz / ⁴⁄₅ cup milk
- 6 ice cubes

SERVES: 2
PREPARATION TIME: 5 MIN

1 . Shell the hazelnuts and crush them with a mortar and pestle.

2 . Toast them in a hot skillet, mixing constantly until they are golden brown.

3 . Put all the ingredients, except the hazelnuts, into the blender and process for about 30 seconds, until you get a frothy mixture.

4 . Sprinkle the milkshakes with toasted hazelnuts.

5 . Serve immediately.

Tips and Tricks

Since you like homemade cooking, try to make your own chocolate spread!
You need: 100 g / 3 ½ oz milk chocolate, 100 g / 3 ½ oz dark chocolate,
2 tablespoons hazelnut butter, 4 tablespoons crème fraîche, 2 tablespoons
water. Melt all the ingredients in a water bath. Cool and enjoy.

46

Fig Jam and Fresh Cheese

1 . Put all the ingredients in the blender.

2 . Process for about 30 seconds, until you get a thick, creamy mixture.

3 . Serve immediately.

- 2 scoops fig sherbet
- 2 petits-suisses, or other rich fromage frais or creamy fresh cheese
- 2 tablespoons
- fig jam (see below recipe)
- 30 cl / 10 fl oz / 1 ¼ cup milk
- 6 ice cubes

SERVES: **2**
PREPARATION TIME: **5** MIN

Fig jam:

- 1 kg / 2.2 lb figs
- 700 g / 1 ½ lb coarse castor sugar
- juice of 1 lemon
- 20 cl / 6 ¾ fl oz / ⁴/5 cup water

MAKES **4** JARS
PREPARATION TIME:
10 MIN
COOKING TIME:
35 MIN

Fig Jam

1 . Wash the figs and pat dry. Cut into quarters, keeping the skin.

2 . Pour the water into a preserving pan, add the sugar and bring to a boil.

3 . Add the fruit and the lemon juice.

4 . Cook over medium heat for 25 minutes, mixing regularly with a large wooden spoon.

5 . Separate into clean jars while still hot and close immediately. Keep in a cool, dry place.

As Lassi

Replace the fig sherbet and the petits-suisses with 2 yogurts or 20 cl / 6 ¾ fl oz / ⁴/5 cup churned buttermilk. Add an additional tablespoon of fig jam.

Liquorice

1 . Melt the liquorice rolls in a saucepan with
30 cl / 10 fl oz / 1 ¼ cup milk.

2 . Remove from heat and cool to room temperature.

3 . Put the melted liquorice and all the other ingredients
into the blender and process for about 30 seconds, until you
get a frothy mixture.

4 . Serve immediately.

- 4 scoops fior
  di latte ice cream
  (see recipe p. 16)
- 4 liquorice rolls
- 1 tablespoon sugar
- 50 cl / 1 pint / 2 cups milk
- 6 ice cubes

SERVES: **2**
PREPARATION TIME: **10** MIN
COOKING TIME: **15** MIN

Did you know?

Who as a child never chewed on liquorice sticks?
Did you know that liquorice can also be used as a natural
medicine? it fights respiratory infections and viruses. But beware,
taken in excessive quantities, liquorice can cause hypertension,
headaches and water retention.

- 4 scoops salt-butter caramel ice cream
- 4 tablespoons salt-butter caramel (see below recipe)
- 20 cl / 6 ¾ fl·oz / ⅘ cup milk
- 6 ice cubes

SERVES: **2**
PREPARATION TIME: **10** MIN

Salt-butter caramel:

- 100 g / 3 ½ oz / ½ cup sugar
- 30 g / 1 oz / ⅛ cup butter
- 3 cl / 1 fl oz / 2 tablespoons crème fraîche or double cream
- 2 cl / ⅔ fl oz / 4 teaspoons water

MAKES **1** JAR
PREPARATION TIME:
5 MIN
COOKING TIME:
10 MIN

Salt-butter Caramel

1 . Put all the ingredients in the blender, with the exception of two tablespoons of salt-butter caramel.

2 . Process for about 30 seconds, until you get a frothy mixture.

3 . Pour a tablespoon of salt-butter caramel into each glass.

4 . Serve immediately.

Salt-butter Caramel

1 . Melt the butter with the water and sugar in a small saucepan.

2 . After about ten minutes, the mixture will begin to brown. Remove from heat and add the crème fraîche.

3 . Cool to room temperature.

4 . You can keep this caramel for several weeks in the refrigerator.

Ingredients

- 2 scoops chocolate ice cream
- 1 banana
- 4 chocolate cookies (see below recipe)
- 2 tablespoons sugar
- 25 cl / 8 ½ fl oz / 1 cup milk
- 6 ice cubes

SERVES: 2
PREPARATION TIME: 5 MIN

Chocolate chip cookies:

- 100 g / 3 ½ oz / scant ½ cup butter
- 100 g / 3 ½ oz / ½ cup sugar
- 200 g / 7 oz / 1 ⅝ cup flour
- 1 egg
- 100 g / 3 ½ oz dark chocolate

MAKES 12 COOKIES
PREPARATION TIME: 10 MIN
SET ASIDE: 1 HR
COOKING TIME: 10 TO 15 MIN

Banana Chocolate

1 . Peel the banana and cut into thick slices.

2 . Place the bananas and all the other ingredients in the blender.

3 . Process for about 30 seconds, until you get a thick, creamy mixture.

4 . Serve immediately.

Chocolate Chip Cookies

1 . Soften the butter over a water bath or in the microwave.

2 . Put the softened butter in a large bowl, add the flour and mix with your fingertips for form small lumps.

3 . Add the sugar and the egg and mix well to get a smooth dough.

4 . Make a ball and set aside for 1 hour.

5 . Preheat the oven to 180°C/350°F/gas mark 4.

6 . Cut the dark chocolate into even pieces.

7 . Divide the dough up into small balls and place them on a baking dish lined with greaseproof paper. Flatten the balls with the palm of your hand.

8 . Place two or three chocolate chunks on each.

9 . Bake for 10 to 15 minutes.

- 4 scoops fior di latte ice cream (see recipe p. 16)
- 12 marshmallows
- 30 cl / 10 fl oz / 1 ¼ cup milk
- 6 ice cubes

SERVES: 2
PREPARATION TIME: 10 MIN
COOKING TIME: 10 MIN

Marshmallow

1 . Melt ten marshmallows with the milk in a saucepan over medium heat. Refrigerate.

2 . Cut the two remaining marshmallows into small pieces.

3 . Put the melted marshmallows with the other ingredients, except the cut marshmallow pieces, into the blender.

4 . Process for about 30 seconds, until you get a thick, creamy mixture.

5 . Sprinkle the milkshake with marshmallow pieces.

6 . Serve immediately.

Twists

You can use other sweets instead of marshmallows, such as fruit gums and foam-based sweets.

As Lassi

Replace the 4 scoops of ice cream with 2 yogurts or 20 cl / 6 ¾ fl oz / ⅘ cup churned buttermilk. Add 2 tablespoons castor sugar.

- 4 scoops fior di latte ice cream (see recipe p. 16)
- 2 tablespoons crispy rice cereal
- 50 g / 1 ¾ oz dark chocolate
- 20 cl / 6 ¾ fl oz / ⁴/₅ cup milk
- 6 ice cubes

SERVES: 2
PREPARATION TIME: 10 MIN

Marshmallow crunch:

- 15 marshmallows
- 50 g / 1 ¾ oz crispy rice cereal
- 15 g / ½ oz / 1 tablespoon butter

MAKES 10 CRUNCHES
PREPARATION TIME:
10 MIN
COOKING TIME:
10 MIN

Chocolate Crunch

1 . Melt 40 g / 1 ½ oz of the dark chocolate in a water bath and pour into the bottom of serving glasses.

2 . Use a vegetable peeler to make slivers out of the remaining chocolate.

3 . Put all the ingredients, except the cereal and the chocolate, into the blender and process for about 30 seconds, until you get a creamy mixture.

4 . Sprinkle with cereal and chocolate shavings.

5 . Serve immediately with marshmallow crunch (see below recipe).

Marshmallow Crunch

1 . Melt the marshmallows with the butter in a saucepan over medium heat.

2 . Add the crispy rice cereal and mix using a spatula.

3 . Make little piles on a piece of greaseproof paper. Cool to room temperature before eating.

- 4 scoops vanilla
  ice cream
- 1 apple, 1 pear
- 2 tablespoons
  rosemary honey
- 1 lump butter
- 20 cl / 6 ¾ fl oz /
  ⅘ cup milk + 6 ice cubes

SERVES: 2 TO 3
PREPARATION TIME: 10 MIN
COOKING TIME: 20 MIN

**Rosemary shortbread
biscuits**

- 150 g / 5 ¼ oz /
  1 ⅕ cup flour
- 70 g / 2 ½ oz /
  ⅓ cup sugar
- 80 g / 2 ⅘ oz / generous
  ⅓ cup butter
- 1 egg, 1 pinch salt
- a few fresh
  rosemary leaves

SERVES: 3
PREPARATION TIME:
10 MIN
COOKING TIME:
15 MIN

Caramel Apple and Pear

1 . Peel the apple and the pear, core them, and cut them
into medium-sized pieces.

2 . Melt the butter in a skillet, add the fruit and then the honey.
Remove from heat after about 20 minutes, when the fruit is cooked
and slightly caramelized. Cool to room temperature.

3 . Place a spoonful of caramelized fruit in each serving glass.
Put all the remaining ingredients into the blender and process
for about 30 seconds, until you get a creamy mixture.

4 . Serve immediately with rosemary shortbread biscuits
(see below recipe).

Rosemary shortbread biscuits

1 . Mix together the flour, sugar and salt in a bowl. Cut the softened butter
into small pieces, add to the flour and work with your fingertips until you
get a sand-like mixture.

2 . Add the rosemary and the egg. Mix together and form into a ball
without kneading it too much. Set it aside at room temperature for one
hour.

3 . Preheat the oven to 180°C/350°F/gas mark 4. Roll out the dough
with a rolling pin on a floured surface until it is three millimetres/an
eighth of an inch thick.

4 . Cut into 10 shortbread biscuits using a cookie cutter of
any shape.

5 . Bake for about 15 minutes.

Ingredients

- 2 yogurts or
  20 cl / 6 ¾ fl oz /
  ⅘ cup churned
  buttermilk
- 1 tablespoon honey
- 1 teaspoon rose water
- a few rose petals
  (optional)
- the seeds from 1 pod
- green cardamom
- 15 cl / 5 fl oz /
  ⅔ cup milk
- 6 ice cubes

SERVES: 2
PREPARATION TIME: 5 MIN

Rose-flavoured Lassi

1 . Crush the green cardamom seeds with a pestle.

2 . Put them with all the other ingredients in the blender.

3 . Process for about 30 seconds, until you get a thick, creamy mixture.

4 . Serve immediately.

Twists

Try with fresh mint leaves instead of cardamom seeds.

Tips and Tricks

Try cardamom to neutralize garlic smells: chew on one after a meal.

Ingredients

- 4 scoops apple sherbet
- 2 Granny Smith apples
- 15 cl / 5 fl oz / ⅔ cup sweet cider
- 10 cl / 3 ⅓ fl oz / ⅖ cup double (heavy) cream
- 6 ice cubes

SERVES: 2 TO 3
PREPARATION TIME: 10 MIN

Butter biscuits

- 200 g / 7 oz / ⅞ cup flour
- 100 g / 3 ½ oz / ½ cup sugar
- 100 g / 3 ½ oz / scant half cup softened salt butter
- 1 egg
- 1 egg yolk

MAKES 20 BISCUITS
PREPARATION TIME:
15 MIN
COOKING TIME:
10 TO 15 MIN

Apple Cider

1 . Peel the apples. Cut them into quarters and core them. Cut into medium-sized pieces.

2 . Put the apples with all the other ingredients in the blender.

3 . Process for about 30 seconds, until you get a creamy mixture.

4 . Serve immediately with butter biscuits (see below recipe).

Butter Biscuits

1 . Mix the butter into the flour by hand, in a large bowl.

2 . Add the sugar and then the whole egg.

3 . Form into a ball and set it aside at room temperature for one hour.

4 . Preheat the oven to 180°C/350°F/gas mark 4.

5 . Shape walnut-sized balls. Place them on a baking sheet lined with greaseproof paper and flatten them.

6 . Brush with egg yolk so the biscuits brown when cooked.

7 . Bake for 10 to 15 minutes.

Ingredients

- 4 scoops lemon sherbet
- 15 cl / 5 fl oz /
  2/3 cup double
  (heavy) cream
- 10 cl / 3 1/3 fl oz /
  2/5 cup limoncello
  (see below recipe)
- 6 ice cubes

SERVES: **6**
PREPARATION TIME: **5** MIN

Limoncello:

- 6 untreated lemon
- 350 g / 12 1/3 oz /
  1 3/4 cup sugar
- 35 cl / 12 fl oz /
  1 1/2 cup 90° alcohol
- 40 cl / 13 1/3 fl oz /
  1 2/3 cup water

MAKES **1** BOTTLE
PREPARATION TIME:
15 MIN
AHEAD OF TIME:
40 DAYS

Lemon Limoncello

1 . Put all the ingredients in the blender.

2 . Process for about 30 seconds, until you get a creamy mixture.

3 . Serve immediately.

Limoncello

1 . Use a vegetable peeler to remove the lemon zest (only the bright yellow surface of the peel).

2 . Mix the lemon zests with the alcohol in a demijohn. Macerate in a dark spot for 40 days.

3 . Strain the liquid and throw away the zests.

4 . Boil the water with the sugar to get a syrup. Remove from heat and cool to room temperature.

5 . Mix the syrup with the alcohol and pour into a pretty bottle.

Ingredients

- 2 scoops coconut ice cream
- 2 scoops pineapple sherbet
- 1 tablespoon cane syrup
- 2 kiwifruit
- 1 mango
- 1 banana
- 10 cl / 3 ⅓ fl oz / ⅖ cup coconut milk
- 10 cl / 3 ⅓ fl oz / ⅖ cup milk
- 5 cl / 1 ⅔ / 3 ⅓ tablespoons rum
- 6 ice cubes

SERVES: 2 TO 3
PREPARATION TIME: 10 MIN

Exotic Rum

1 . Peel the fruit. Cut the mango in two and remove the pit. Cut the fruit into medium-sized pieces.

2 . Put them with all the other ingredients in the blender.

3 . Process for about 30 seconds, until you get a thick, creamy mixture.

4 . Serve immediately.

Did you know?

Did you know that the kiwifruit tree is in the genus Actinidia and grows wild in China, in the Yangze River Valley. Cultivation spread in the early twentieth century. Today, the top kiwi producers in the world are Italy, New Zealand, Chile and France.

Ingredients

- 4 scoops nougat ice cream
- 30 pitted Morello cherries
- 2 tablespoons cherry jam
- 2 tablespoons cherry liqueur
- 20 cl / 6 ¾ fl oz / ⅘ cup milk
- 6 ice cubes

SERVES: 2
PREPARATION TIME: 5 MIN

Liqueur cherries:

- 1 kg / 2.2 lbs Morello cherries
- 250 g / 9 oz / 1 ¼ cup sugar
- 1 l / 2 pints / 4 ¼ cups clear brandy (45°)

MAKES 6 JARS
PREPARATION TIME: 10 MIN
SET ASIDE: 2 MONTHS

Cherry Liqueur

1 . Put all the ingredients in the blender.

2 . Process for about 30 seconds, until you get a creamy mixture.

3 . Serve with Liqueur cherries (see below recipe), dipped in melted chocolate.

Liqueur Cherries

1 . Wash and pat the cherries dry.

2 . Cut the stems down to one centimetre (a third of an inch).

3 . Layer the cherries in jars, alternating with the sugar. Close the jars and macerate in the sun for 48 hours.

4 . Cover the cherries with the brandy, close the jars and store then in a cool, dark place.

5 . Turn the jars every week to mix the sugar well.

6 . Wait at least two months before eating them!

Ingredients

- 5 small tomatoes
- 150 g fresh sheep's milk cheese
- 6 basil leaves
- 5 cl / 1 ⅔ fl oz / 3 ⅓ tablespoons milk
- 6 ice cubes
- celery salt
- pepper

SERVES: 6
PREPARATION TIME: 10 MIN
COOKING TIME: 3 MIN

Parmesan lollies:

- 6 teaspoons grated parmesan cheese
- 6 wooden skewers

MAKES 6 LOLLIES
PREPARATION TIME: 5 MIN
COOKING TIME: 5 MIN

Tomato and Basil

1 . Peel the tomatoes: bring water to a boil (enough to cover the tomatoes entirely), and dip the tomatoes in the boiling water for 3 minutes, then run them immediately under cold water. Peel the tomatoes, cut them in half and remove the seeds.

2 . Clean the basil leaves.

3 . Place the tomatoes, basil and all the other ingredients in the blender. Process for about 30 seconds, until you get a creamy mixture.

4 . Serve immediately, as an appetizer, with parmesan lollies (see below recipe).

Parmesan Lollies

1 . Preheat the oven to 200°C/400°F/gas mark 6.

2 . Line a baking dish with greaseproof paper and make six small piles of parmesan cheese, well spaced from each other. Place a wooden skewer coming out of each pile to form a lolly.

3 . Bake until golden brown (around 5 minutes)

4 . Cool to room temperature before eating. You can store these lollies in a metal box for several days.

Mint Cucumber

- 1 small cucumber (about 300 g / 10 ½ oz)
- ½ clove garlic
- 1 sprig parsley
- 5 mint leaves
- 1 yogurt
- 10 cl / 3 ⅓ fl oz / ⅖ cup milk
- 6 ice cubes
- pepper
- salt

SERVES: **6**
PREPARATION TIME: **5** MIN

1 . Peel the cucumber, remove the seeds and cut into medium-sized pieces. Peel the garlic and chop. Wash the parsley and mint and chop.

2 . Put the cucumber, garlic, parley and mint with all the other ingredients into the blender.

3 . Process for about 30 seconds, until you get a frothy mixture.

4 . Serve immediately as an appetizer with large raisins and shrimp skewers dipped in gomashio (a mixture of toasted sesame pounded with sea salt).

Did you know?

Did you know that cucumbers are used in cosmetics? At home, you can use them to calm itching and irritations: just apply the cucumber directly to the skin. For sunburn, mix the juice of one cucumber with two tablespoons milk and spread this mixture on the burn.

Tips and Tricks

To make cucumbers easier to digest, take the time to sprinkle with salt and leave to drain. First, cut them in slices, then cover with rock salt. Leave them to drain for a few hours. Then rinse and dry the cucumbers before using them.

Ingredients

- 1 large tomato, peeled
- 1/4 green bell pepper
- 1/4 cucumber
- 1/2 sweet onion
- 1/2 clove garlic
- 5 mint leaves
- 10 cl / 3 1/3 fl oz / 2/5 cup milk
- 1 tablespoon olive oil
- 1/2 teaspoon balsamic vinegar
- 2 drops Tabasco sauce
- 6 ice cubes and salt

SERVES: **6**
PREPARATION TIME: **10** MIN
COOKING TIME: **3** MIN

Pine nut crumble:

- 50 g / 1 3/4 oz / 1/2 cup pine nuts (or almond slivers)
- 1 thick slice country-style bread
- 1 clove garlic

SERVES: **6**
PREPARATION TIME: **5** MIN
COOKING TIME: **5** MIN

Gazpacho

1 . Peel the tomato: bring water to a boil and dip the tomatoes in the boiling water for 3 minutes, then run them immediately under cold water. Peel the tomato, cut it in half and remove the seeds.

2 . Peel the cucumber, the garlic and the onion. Remove the stem and seeds of the green pepper. Then cut them all into medium-sized pieces.

3 . Wash a few mint leaves.

4 . Place all these ingredients with the other ingredients in the blender.

5 . Process for about 30 seconds, until you get a frothy mixture.

6 . Just before serving, sprinkle with pine nut crumble and grilled almonds (see below recipe).

7 . Serve immediately.

Pine Nut Crumble

1 . Toast the pine nuts or almonds in a skillet for about five minutes (without any fat).

2 . Toast the slice of bread in a toaster.

3 . Rub it with the garlic clove, crush in a mortar with the pine nuts to make the crumble.

As Lassi

Replace the 10 cl / 3 1/3 fl oz / 2/5 cup milk with 15 cl / 5 fl oz / 2/3 cup churned buttermilk.

Ingredients

- 2 fennel bulbs
- 150 g / 5 ¼ oz / ²/₃ cup flour
- 6 ice cubes
- pepper
- salt

SERVES: **6**
PREPARATION TIME: **5** MIN

Smoked salmon *involtini*:

- 3 slices smoked salmon
- 60 g / 5 oz / ¹/₃ cup ricotta
- 12 fennel sprigs
- juice of 1 lemon (optional)

MAKES **12** *INVOLTINI*
PREPARATION TIME: **5** MIN

Fennel and Ricotta

1. Clean the fennel and remove the stringy parts. Juice them in a centrifuge juicer.

2. Put 30 cl / 10 fl oz / 1 ¼ cup fennel juice with the other ingredients in the blender.

3. Process for about 30 seconds, until you get a frothy mixture.

4. Serve immediately, as an appetizer, with smoked salmon *involtini* (see below recipe).

Smoked Salmon Involtini

1. Cut each salmon slice into four rectangles.

2. Put a dollop of ricotta and a sprig of fennel in the centre of each rectangle.

3. Close each rectangle with a toothpick. Sprinkle with lemon juice if you want.

Did you know?

Fennel has many virtues! It heals earaches and stomach and colon pain, it fights wind, calms toothaches, rheumatism and asthma, is good for ailments of the upper respiratory system and promotes lactation. It is clearly a tonic!

Cream Cheese and Mint

1 . Clean the mint leaves and dry them. Peel the garlic.

2 . Put the mint and garlic with all the other ingredients in the blender.

3 . Process for about 30 seconds, until you get a frothy mixture.

4 . Serve immediately, as an appetizer or to accompany a starter, such as a savoury tart.

Tips and Tricks

Did you know that if you throw a few fresh mint leaves in a vase, your bouquet will last longer? If you live in a flat, grow mint on your balcony. This robust plant proliferates! You don't have to start from seed. Instead, get yourself a few stems and put them in a glass of water until they form roots. Then you can plant them.

- 4 squares fresh cream cheese
- 4 tablespoons mint leaves
- ½ clove garlic
- 20 cl / 6 ¾ fl oz / ⅘ cup milk
- 6 ice cubes
- pepper
- salt

SERVES: 6
PREPARATION TIME: 5 MIN

As Lassi

Replace the cream cheese with 2 yogurts or 20 cl / 6 ¾ fl oz / ⅘ cup churned buttermilk. Use 5 cl / 1 ⅔ fl oz / 3 ⅓ tablespoons less milk.

- 1 ripe avocado
- 2 sheep's milk yogurts
- 10 sprigs chives
- 4 drops Tabasco sauce
- juice of 1/2 lemon
- 20 cl/6 3/4 fl oz/ 4/5 cup milk
- 6 ice cubes
- pepper
- salt

SERVES: 6
PREPARATION TIME: 5 MIN

Avocado Lassi

1 . Peel the avocado and remove the pit. Clean the chives and chop them up roughly.

2 . Put the avocado and chives with all the other ingredients in the blender.

3 . Process for about 30 seconds, until you get a thick, creamy mixture.

4 . Serve immediately, as an appetizer or to accompany a shrimp-based starter, for example.

Did you know?

Avocados have a lot of calories (140 kilocalories for 100 g/3 1/2 oz). It is particularly rich in monounsaturated lipids, which are good for the cardiovascular system and blood circulation, and they also have vitamin B and E, which help fight ageing.

Tips and Tricks

Prefer avocados that are still hard, when you choose them in the store; this is a sign that they are fresh. In fact, they ripen once they have been picked, in contact with ethylene, a gas that is found in air. To ripen avocados faster, store them with bananas or apples, which naturally give off ethylene. Avoid cutting open avocados too far in advance, as they oxidise in contact with the air. Counter this by rubbing them with lemon juice. Never put them near citrus fruit, as this will cause them to brown.

Ingredients

- 2 slices watermelon
- 50 g / 1 ¾ oz / ⅓ cup feta
- 2 yogurts
- 10 sprigs chives
- 6 ice cubes
- 10 turns of a pepper mill
- salt

SERVES: 6
PREPARATION TIME: 5 MIN

Pepper Watermelon Lassi with Feta

1 . Remove the rind of the watermelon along with any seeds. Cut into a large dice.
2 . Clean the chives and chop them up roughly.
3 . Put the watermelon and the chives with all the other ingredients in the blender.
4 . Process for about 30 seconds, until you get a frothy mixture.
5 . Serve immediately, preferably as an appetizer.

Twists

Try adding a tablespoon of balsamic vinegar to your milkshake.

Tips and Tricks

Choose seedless watermelon to save time. If you only find one with seeds, keep the latter and toast them with a little salt. They are delicious with drinks.

Ingredients

- 200 g / 7 oz fresh broad beans
- 100 g / 3 ⅓ oz / scant half cup fromage blanc or yogurt cheese
- 3 tablespoons chervil
- 20 cl / 6 ¾ fl oz / ⁴⁄₅ cup milk + 6 ice cubes
- salt and pepper

SERVES: 6

PREPARATION TIME: 10 MIN

Comté cheese puffs:

- 25 cl / 8 ½ fl oz / 1 cup water
- 90 g / 3 ⅕ oz / ⅜ cup butter
- 150 g / 5 ¼ oz / 1 ⅕ cup flour
- 4 eggs
- 75 g / 2 ½ oz / ¾ cup grated comté cheese
- salt and pepper

MAKES 20 PUFFS

PREPARATION TIME: 10 MIN

SET ASIDE: 15 MIN

COOKING TIME: 15 MIN

Broad Bean and Chervil

1 . Cook the broad beans in boiling water for 1 minute.

2 . Cool them in ice water and then remove the skin.

3 . Wash the chervil and chop.

4 . Put the broad beans and the chervil with all the other ingredients in the blender.

5 . Process for about 30 seconds, until you get a frothy mixture.

6 . Serve immediately, as an appetizer, with the comté cheese puffs (see below recipe).

Comté Cheese Puffs

1 . Bring the butter and water to a boil in a saucepan. Season with salt and pepper.

2 . Add the flour and dry the mixture over a low heat for about 10 minutes; the dough should come away from the edges of the pan.

3 . Cool to room temperature.

4 . Preheat the oven to 200°C/400°F/gas mark 6.

5 . Add the eggs one by one and then the grated comté cheese.

6 . Use a spoon to for small piles on a baking dish lined with greaseproof paper.

7 . Bake for 15 minutes.

Greek-style Beetroot Lassi

1 . Cook the sweet potato in boiling salted water for about 10 minutes. Drain and cool to room temperature.

2 . Peel the onion and cut in half.

3 . Put all the ingredients in the blender.

4 . Process for about 30 seconds, until you get a creamy mixture.

5 . Serve immediately, as an appetizer, with the beetroot crisps (see below recipe).

- 300 g / 10 ½ oz cooked beetroot
- 1 small sweet potato (50 g / 1 ¾ oz)
- ½ small onion
- 1 Greek-style yogurt
- a hint Cayenne pepper
- 30 cl / 10 fl oz / 1 ¼ cup milk
- 6 ice cubes
- pepper
- salt

SERVES: **6**
PREPARATION TIME: **10** MIN
COOKING TIME: **10** MIN

Beetroot crisps:

- 2 raw beetroots
- oil for frying
- salt

MAKES **30** CRISPS
PREPARATION TIME: **5** MIN
COOKING TIME: **3** MIN

Beetroot Crisps

1 . Clean the beetroots, peel them and cut them into thin slices using a mandoline.

2 . Heat the oil for frying. Drop in the beetroot slices and fry for 3 minutes.

3 . Remove them and drain on paper towels. Salt.

4 . Cool to room temperature.

Tips and Tricks

Did you know that beetroot is delicious raw? Grate with carrot and a small sweet onion and you get a beautiful and flavourful starter!

Greens and Sprout Lassi

1 . Clean the greens and spin dry.

2 . Peel the half avocado and remove the pit.
Cut into two pieces.

3 . Put all the ingredients, except the sprouts, in the blender.

4 . Process for about 30 seconds, until you get a creamy mixture.

5 . Sprinkle the milkshakes with the germs.

6 . Serve immediately, as an appetizer or to accompany a starter.

- 2 handfuls young greens
  (spinach, rocket, mesclun)
- 1/2 avocado
- 1 sheep's milk yogurt
- 2 tablespoons sprouts
- 1 tablespoon lemon juice
- 6 ice cubes
- pepper
- salt

SERVES: 6
PREPARATION TIME: 10 MIN

Tips and Tricks

Make your own sprouts: they are a goldmine of vitamins and minerals! Get yourself a sprouting receptacle (available in health food stores). Choose a variety of seeds to sprout (the same stores carry various mixtures of seeds for sprouting). Put the seeds in the sprouting receptacle, wash them two or three times a day and watch them grow! You can eat them after five or ten days, depending on the seed.

Ginger and Cumin Carrot

- 3 carrots
- 50 g/1 ¾ oz fresh goat cheese
- 1 small piece fresh ginger
- 1 pinch ground ginger
- 1 pinch ground cumin
- 6 ice cubes
- pepper
- salt

SERVES: **6**
PREPARATION TIME: **10** MIN

1 . Peel and wash the carrots. Juice them in a centrifuge juicer.

2 . Do the same with the ginger.

3 . Put 25 cl / 8 ½ fl oz / 1 cup carrot juice and the ginger juice with the other ingredients in the blender.

4 . Process for about 30 seconds, until you get a frothy mixture.

5 . Serve immediately, as an appetizer or to accompany a cheese-based starter, for exampltte.

Did you know?

Ginger is a tropical plant from India related to the orchid. For Indians, this is very basic plant and a universal remedy. Ginger helps nausea and vomiting caused by motion sickness, seasickness and pregnancy. It relieves minor digestive troubles, intestinal spasms, colic and gas. It helps fight the symptoms of colds and flu, migraine headaches and rheumatism pain.

Recipe Index

Acknowledgements

The author thanks Anna, Pénélope and Lucie Duval,
Christel Cousin and Anne-Françoise Majault,
Monique and Hervé Le Hingrat.

Editorial Director: Muriel Villebrun
Editorial coordination: Béatrice Cordonnier
Editing: Laure-Hélène Accaoui
Graphic design: Valérie Ferrer
Translation: Anne Trager

Photoengraving: Photogravure du Pays d'Oc,
Nîmes, France
Printing and binding: Delo Tiskarna, Slovenia, Europe

British Library Cataloguing in Publication Data available
ISBN n° 978-1-906909-06-2

Romain Pages Éditions
BP 82 030
30 252 Sommières Cedex
France
email: contact@romain-pages.com
web site: www.romain-pages.com

Romain Pages Publishing
Lincoln House – 300 High Holborn
London WC1V 7JH
United Kingdom
email: enquiries@romain-pages.co.uk
web site: www.romain-pages.co.uk